The Secret Fort

by Juanita Havill

illustrated by
Thomas Sperling

MODERN CURRICULUM PRESS

Pearson Learning Group

Emily ran home from the bus stop. There was nothing unusual about that. Emily loved to run. She had been the fastest runner in fifth grade in her old school. She didn't know yet if that would happen at her new school. She had only been there a week.

She didn't feel comfortable at school yet. Now she was the only deaf student in class. Before, her best friend Nell was deaf too, and they had signed to have a conversation. Her teacher at her old school had signed. Emily hadn't needed an interpreter. Now she had an interpreter, Mrs. Simpson. She was nice, but Emily wished some of the kids could sign too.

Emily ran into the house and headed for the family room. Her older sister Lisa sat at the computer. Emily was disappointed. She wanted to have a computer conversation with Nell.

Lisa jumped when Emily tapped her on the shoulder. She signed to tell her she wanted to e-mail Nell.

"No way, Emily. I've got a report due," Lisa said.

Emily read her lips. Lisa knew how to sign, but sometimes she was lazy. Mom and Dad were hearing too, but they always signed to Emily.

3

Lisa gestured toward the door, and Emily stomped off, frustrated. Then she barged back into the room to tell Lisa she was going out running. Lisa nodded and off went Emily, out the back door, up the long backyard, and along a path beside a cornfield. Their new house was at the edge of town.

Emily liked running beside the cornfield. She didn't have to watch all the time for city traffic, which she couldn't hear.

Emily ran quickly. As she came to a woods beside the cornfield, she slowed down to peer into it. There was a broken, rotting fence. Emily decided to take a break and explore.

It was cool under the trees. Some of the maples
had changed colors. Bright orange and red leaves
lay scattered across the ground. Emily breathed in the
wonderful, spicy, dried-leaf smell of fall. Then she saw
a large broken branch hanging to the ground. The
branch was still attached to a tree, and that gave
Emily an idea.

As fast as she could, Emily ran back to the cornfield and gathered a dozen sturdy dried cornstalks. She took them to the broken branch and leaned them against it to make a shelter. She fastened the stalks together with corn leaves. "I need more," she said to herself, and went back to the fields. When she had a wall of stalks, she brushed dried leaves onto the floor and crawled into her new fort to sit and think for a while.

That night Emily e-mailed Nell to tell her about the fort. "It's the best hideout ever. I wish you were here," she wrote. She was going to type more, but her dad came in the room and gestured toward the window. Emily could see lightning. It had started to storm, so she shut off the computer.

The next day Emily raced to her fort right after school. She took some comic books and a bottle of juice to store there.

She stopped short when she saw her fort. The corn stalks had been ripped from the fallen branch, and her leaf carpet was thin and patchy. Had someone come and torn her fort apart? Then she remembered the storm last night.

Instead of giving up, Emily decided to build another, stronger fort. She ran back home and got some old wood, a hammer, and nails from the garage. She found a large piece of canvas. It would make a great roof.

Emily got some crackers, another bottle of juice, more comics, and her favorite science fiction trilogy. Then she placed everything in an old wagon.

When she reached the branch, she went to work. She nailed the boards to the dead branch, then fastened the canvas over them. Inside the fort she made a shelf for her books with two boards and some rocks. Once again she piled leaves onto the floor. She left her food supplies under the shelf.

No storm would blow this fort down. Emily was sure of that.

The rest of the week she went to the fort after
school. She even did her homework there. On the
weekend she took a little stool to the fort along with a
plastic carton for her books. If it stormed, she wanted
to be sure her books would stay dry.

On Monday, just as she entered the woods, she
saw a squirrel dashing away from the clearing. Then
a dozen blackbirds flew toward her out of the woods.
Someone else was in there.

Emily crept toward the clearing. She caught sight of two girls and hid behind a bush to watch them. One girl with long black hair and a red windbreaker was in her class at school. Emily didn't recognize the other one. She had short brown hair and a blue jacket.

Emily tried to follow their conversation. But she wasn't close enough to read their lips well.

Most of the boards had been pulled off the branch and lay in a heap. The brown-haired girl gestured toward the ground and Emily saw the plastic box on its side. Her books looked as if someone had tossed them into the air. Some of the cracker packages were open and lying on the ground.

Emily felt anger pound in her chest. Had those two girls wrecked her fort? She watched them pick up the books carefully and stack them by the branch. They found the lid for the plastic box and put the cracker packages inside it before snapping the lid on.

Emily leaned forward. A branch that she held in her hand broke off. She could feel the branch snap and was sure the girls had heard it. They stopped and looked her way. The brown-haired girl shouted something, but Emily couldn't catch it.

Emily stood up and walked toward them. She didn't know what to expect. It wasn't always easy to have a conversation with hearing people without an interpreter. And she wasn't sure what these kids were up to. She gestured toward the fort and then pointed to herself.

The black-haired girl turned to her friend. "Karen, she's the new kid at school. She's deaf, remember?"

The brown-haired girl said something about the fort and private property. Emily could barely read her lips because she was shouting. Emily gave up and leaned down to pick up the boards. The black-haired girl walked over to help.

When the canvas was laid out flat with the boards on it, the girl said, "My name is Sally and this is Karen. Too bad about your fort."

Emily stared at her fort. She was glad Sally and Karen hadn't done it, but she couldn't stop a sad feeling from welling up when she looked at the place. It was a wreck.

She felt a hand on her shoulder and turned to look at Sally. Sally pointed to the litter of boards, then gestured to all three of them. She pretended to build something, and Emily knew she was offering to help. Karen told them they should build the fort on the other side of the fence. She said the man who owned this property hadn't wanted the fort there. Karen explained that the man had often told kids not to go on his property. They carried everything to the edge of the cornfield.

"This field belongs to my uncle," Karen said. "He won't mind our building the fort here."

The girls put the fort together again. They built it teepee style around a tree with a small trunk.

Emily invited the girls over and set off running. They followed, but had trouble keeping up.

"You're fast!" Sally said when they got to Emily's. "You should be on the track team with us."

That night Emily sent an e-mail to Nell. "I built a new fort today. Some old man tore down the other one, I think. I goofed and built it on his property. Sally and Karen helped me. They're some girls at school. It's a neat fort."

The next night Emily wrote another note to Nell. "Things are looking up. I made some friends who are on the track team here. And I'm going to try out for it. Wish me luck!"

⊙ **Comprehension Skill:** Understanding Character

Modern Curriculum Press edition, 2004

ISBN 0-7652-3467-X

Printed in the United States of America

2 3 4 5 6 7 8 9 10   10 09 08

Pearson Learning Group

1-800-321-3106
www.pearsonlearning.com

COMPREHENSION POWER READERS

Power Reader #21

Comprehension Skill:
Understanding
Character

Genre: Realistic Story

DRA	38
Guided Reading	P
Lexile	610

1-800-321-3106
www.pearsonlearning.com

Modern
Curriculum
Press
Pearson Learning Group

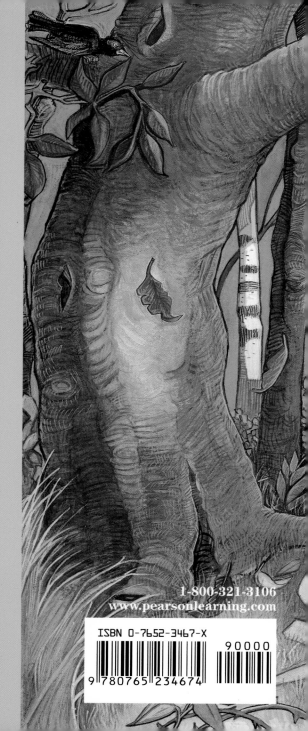

RUSTY'S SONG

by Milo Mason
illustrated by Lee Lee Brazeal